READY OR NOT
HERE I COME

READY OR NOT HERE I COME

Dennis King

Tampa, Florida

The views and opinions expressed in this book are solely those of the author and do not reflect the views or opinions of Gatekeeper Press. Gatekeeper Press is not to be held responsible for and expressly disclaims responsibility for the content herein.

Ready or Not Here I Come

Published by Gatekeeper Press
7853 Gunn Hwy, Suite 209
Tampa, FL 33626
www.GatekeeperPress.com

Copyright © 2023 by Dennis King

All rights reserved. Neither this book, nor any parts within it may be sold or reproduced in any form or by any electronic or mechanical means, including information storage and retrieval systems, without permission in writing from the author. The only exception is by a reviewer, who may quote short excerpts in a review.

The cover design, interior formatting, typesetting, and editorial work for this book are entirely the product of the author. Gatekeeper Press did not participate in and is not responsible for any aspect of these elements.

ISBN (paperback): 9781662939501

Table of Contents

Introduction	3
1. God So Loved the World	5
2. Work It Out	9
3. Ready Or Not Here I Come	19
4. Receive Me Now	27
5. Trials and Tribulations	31
6. Victory In Jesus	41
Special Thanks	53

Introduction

The purpose of this book is to equip God's people with the simplistic word of God. To reach that person who does not believe in the Lord, or the person who doesn't know what to believe. The word of God says "Enter by the narrow gate; for wide is the gate and broad is the way that leads to destruction, and there are many who go in by it. Because narrow is the gate and difficult is the way which leads to life, and there are few who find it." Matthew 7:13- 14. This book is for them. The Lord will show himself in the clouds one day and call His people home to heaven. This event is called the rapture of the Church. There will be those who miss that event, because of unbelief. They will have one more opportunity to be saved, but it will come at a terrible price during tribulation period. To the reader of this book, now is the time to make a decision to accept Christ in your heart. Don't gamble with your soul. I have a burden in my heart to create this booklet for my loved ones, and to encourage all people to receive Christ as savior before the rapture and the terrible 7-year tribulation period.

1. God So Loved the world

God was disappointed with the first man and first woman, Adam and Eve. He made paradise and placed them in the midst of it. Everything they could ever want and need was there for them. No sickness, hurt or pain only love and peace. In Genesis 1 and 2 we see the creation of heaven and earth, man and women. In Genesis 3:11-19, God shows His disappointment with man. They could do no wrong up to this point, but now their eyes were open, eyes that God wanted to keep closed. This was to be the age of innocence. God began to deal with the serpent that deceived them. Then Eve and next Adam. God planned a life for mankind that was perfect. All we had to do was obey. He had every reason to be upset with his creation, man, but in Genesis 3:21, His love and compassion immediately kicks in and He starts to provide for his kids, and he loves them right where they are. Verse 21: reads "Also for Adam and his wife the Lord God made tunics of skin, and clothed them." There are many times in the Old Testament where man has fallen short and just flat out disobeyed Gods word. In "Ephesians 4:2 the Lord asked that we bear with one another in love. God would never ask us to do or to be something we couldn't. No matter what you have done in life, or what you've been through, our Lord and Savior is a master at loving you. John 3:16 God gives us His most prized possession. "For God so loved the world that he gave His only begotten Son, that whoever believes in Him should not perish but have everlasting Life." That is why I'm writing this book because no matter where you are in life, no matter what you have done, God, the creator of heaven and earth, wants to spend eternity with you. After the fall of man the only way to redeem man was to give his Son as a sin offering. John 3:16. The thing I like about our Lord and Savior is He is always thinking of us, whether we are being blessed or going through a trial. It's always about building character in us and changing us into the image of his Son.

I understand my ministry more and more everyday, and that is to encourage people to be a part of Gods family. When you are part of a family there are benefits attached, protection, provision, and love. In John 14:2-3 Jesus said "In My Father's house are many mansions; if it were not so I would have told you, I go to prepare a place for you. And if I go and prepare a place for you, I will come again and receive you to myself; that where I am, you may be also." The Bible tells us that God knows the beginning and the end. And he knows every hair on our head. There is a time coming when the Lord is going to draw a line in the sand and He wants you to be on the right side of that line. He knows you better than you know yourself, and wants to spend eternity with you.

2. Work it out

In my walk as a Christian, I've always looked at God as being perfect, all knowing all loving and never wrong, and if He's never wrong, then the problem is with us. Yes, I fall short, way short. I received the Lord as my Savior on November 24, 1985 and was baptized on Easter the following year. In the 27 years that I've been a believer the lord has delivered me from many things: drugs, alcohol, cigarettes, just to name a few. The truth is, no matter how clean I think I am, I'm just a sinner saved by Grace. Romans 3:23 reads "for all have sinned and fall short of the glory of God." Jesus is the only way to the Father. We can never be good enough. We can't earn something that has been freely given to us. We can only receive the gift or reject the gift. Sadly to say that's what many will do, reject God's loving gift, Jesus Christ. The following scriptures show how our pride and selfishness can get in the way of our salvation.

1. "There is a way that seams right to a man, but in the end it leads to death." (Separation from God) Proverbs 14:12
2. "For what profit is it to a man if he gains the whole world, and lose his own soul? Or what will a man give in exchange for his soul." Matthew 16:26

When we die our soul will go somewhere, to heaven if we receive Jesus as our lord and savior, Ephesians 1:3 and Ephesians 2:6, or to hell, the place of the wicked if we reject Jesus as our Lord. Luke 12:4-7 tells us to fear God to respect him as creator. Luke 16:19-31 tells the story of two men, one who believed and one who didn't. It reads: "There was a certain rich man who was clothed in purple and fine linen and fared sumptuously every day. But there was a certain beggar named Lazarus, full of sores, who was laid at his gate, desiring to be fed with the crumbs which fell from the rich man's table. Moreover the dogs came and licked his sores. So it was that the beggar died, and was carried by the angels to Abraham's bosom. The rich man also died and was buried. And being in torments in Hades, he lifted up his eyes and saw Abraham afar off, and Lazarus in his bosom. Then he cried and said, 'Father Abraham, have mercy on me, and send Lazarus that he may dip the tip of his finger in water and cool my tongue; for I am tormented in this flame.' but Abraham said, 'Son, remember that in your lifetime you received your good things, and likewise Lazarus evil things; but now he is comforted and you are tormented. And besides all this, between us and you there is a great gulf fixed, so that those who want to pass from here to you cannot, nor can those from there pass to us. Then he said, 'I beg you therefore, father, that you would send him to my father's house, for I have five brothers, that he may testify to them, lest they also come to this place of torment.' Abraham said to him, 'They have Moses and the prophets; let them hear them.' and he said, 'No, father Abraham; but if one goes to them from the dead, they will repent,' But he said to him, 'If they do not hear Moses and the Prophets, neither will they be persuaded through one rise from the dead."

This is so true, Jesus rose from the dead, Matthew 28:1-6, and is standing at the right hand of God. Acts 7:55. He gave his life for you. We have his word, the Bible, His living word. We have men of God preaching and teaching in our churches, on TV and radio. Our Lord has given us everything that pertains to life and Godliness.

God never intended for man to go to hell. He created it for Satan and the fallen angles that forfeited the heavenly experience, but because man chooses to follow Satan (evil) instead of Jesus (holiness) God has no other choice. Our Lord and Savior is telling us to get off the fence. There is no neutral stand when it comes to your belief. You didn't create yourself, (you were created by God). **To not make a choice for Jesus, means you have made a choice for Satan.**

The following scriptures reveal more awesome truths about the reality of life and that we are not in control of our stay here on earth. Sure we take care of our bodies, live holy, eat right and prolong some things, but accidents do happen. There are so many variables to keep in mind. The Bible said in James 4:14 "whereas you do not know what will happen tomorrow. For what is your life? It is even a vapor that appears for a little time and then vanishes away."

Another reality is God may simply say enough is enough. Don't think for one second he won't. He's done it before. Let's take a look at Genesis 6:5- 6 "Then the Lord saw that the wickedness of man was great in the earth, and that every intent of the thoughts of his heart was only evil continually. And the lord was sorry that He had made man on the earth, and He was grieved in his Heart. In Genesis 6:13 God takes the next step. "And God said to Noah, "The end of all flesh has come before me, for the earth is filled with violence through them; and behold, I will destroy them with the earth."

What I am saying to you is, God has a plan; He will not kill everyone on earth, but He is going to clean some things up. Our Heavenly Father loves us and he wants to restore things, this earth and us. I restore motorcycles as a hobby, and when

I start a project I strip all parts off the bike so I can get to everything. Parts that are rusty or bent have to be sanded, painted and fixed. Other parts have to be replaced altogether. The point I am making is this, that things really look bad during this process, but when I am finished it's all shiny and new. That's the same with God. His word tells us in Acts 3:19-21 that there is restoration coming. "Repent therefore and be converted, that your sins may be blotted out, so that times of refreshing may come from the presence of the Lord, and that He may send Jesus Christ who was preached to you before, whom heaven must receive until the time of restoration of all things, which God has spoken by the mouth of all His holy prophets since the world began." In Colossians 1:19-20 Gods word said "For it pleased the Father that in Him all the fullness should dwell, and by Him to reconcile all things to himself, by Him whether things on earth or things in heaven, having made peace through the blood of

His cross." At some point, God will send his Son to bring true believers of Christ into heaven. You will find this in 1 Thessalonians 4:13-18. Verses 16-17 said, "For the Lord Himself will descend from heaven with a shout, with the trumpet of God. And the dead in Christ will rise first. Then we who are alive and remain shall be caught up together with them in the clouds to meet the Lord in the air. And thus we shall always be with the Lord."

In Verse 18, scripture tells us to comfort one another with these words. If you are not comforted by His word or you are not sure where you stand with God right now, Romans 10:9 said "That if you confess with your mouth the Lord Jesus and believe in your heart that God has raised Him from the dead, **you will be saved.**" Say the prayer below and mean it with all of your heart, and become a member God's family, and allow the restoration of God to take place in your life.

I confess with my mouth that Jesus is Lord and that He died on the cross for my sins, and I believe in my heart that God raised him from the dead on the third day for my justification; I do now receive Him as my Lord and savior. Amen

Congratulations! If you made that first step, the Lord has just forgiven you from every sin you have ever committed. Psalm 103:12, Jeremiah 31:34, and Hebrews 10:17, and now wants to love you right where you are at. It's easy in the age of grace to make a decision for Christ, but after the Rapture of the Church, things will change drastically. The seven-year tribulation will start; the whole earth will experience deception, by the enemy of our soul, making it vary difficult to know a lie from the truth.

3. Ready or Not Here I Come

It is important you realize that the saints being caught up to meet the Lord in the air in 1 Thessalonians 4:17 is not the same event as the second coming of the Lord in Revelations 19:11-21. The second coming of Christ is an event all by itself. It will happen after the rapture of the Church and bring an end to the Great Tribulation Period. God will remove true believers in Christ in the rapture. Then the world will go through judgment (seven years of tribulations). Jesus will return on a white horse with armies from heaven clothed in white to strike the nations to put an end to the evil brought on by kings of the earth and the Beast and the False Prophet. This is called the Second Coming of Christ.

The event that the Bible calls the rising or catching away of saints is no new concept for God. The Old Testament has evidence of God performing this great miracle more then once. The two Old Testament saints that I'm referring to were special in God's eye, Like You, and did not have to experience death to go to heaven. They were Enoch and Elijah. Let's look at Enoch in Genesis 5. The Bible breaks down the families of Adam and goes on to tell us how long they lived, but when it gets to Enoch something different happens. Let's take a look. Genesis 5:17-24 reads "So the days of Mahalalel were eight hundred and ninety-five years; and he died, Jared lived one hundred and sixty-two years, and begot Enoch. After he begot Enoch, Jared lived eight hundred years, and had sons and daughters. So all the days of Jared were nine hundred and sixty-two years; and he died. Enoch lived sixty-five years, and begot Methuselah. After he begot Methuselah, Enoch walked with God three hundred years, and had sons and daughters. So all the days of Enoch were three hundred and sixty-five years. And Enoch walked with God; and he was not, for God took him."

The Lord God backs his word up in Hebrews 11:5 and it reads "By faith Enoch was taken away so that he did not see death, "and was not found, because God had taken him"; for before he was taken he had this testimony, that he pleased God."

How can we have the same testimony Enoch had? By receiving Jesus Christ as Lord and Savior, Jesus then sees us as a finished work, as one who walks with God.

Now let's take a look at Elijah's experience. 2 Kings 2:1 reads "And it came to pass, when the Lord was about to take up Elijah into heaven by a whirlwind, that Elijah went with Elisha from Gilgal. Verses 11-12 reads. "Then it happened, as they continued on and talked, that suddenly a chariot of fire appeared with horses of fire, and separated the two of them; and Elijah went up by a whirlwind into heaven. And Elisha saw it, and cried out, "My father, my father, the chariot of Israel and its horsemen!" So he saw him no more. And he took hold of his own clothes and tore them into two pieces.

Elijah had a prophetic ministry that could call fire down from heaven and was known as a Man of God. Just like us, Elisha had prior knowledge that Elijah was going to ascend to heaven, 2 Kings 2:3. What will you do with the word God has given you? Elisha witnessed this whole event. Will you be someone who witnesses this event? Or will you be someone who takes part in the event?

At some point God will start this process of restoring things. No man knows when the Lord Jesus will appear in the clouds, but Matthew 24:36-44 reads "But of that day and hour no one knows, not even the angels of heaven, but Father only. But as in the days of Noah were, so also will the coming of the Son of Man be. For as in the days before the flood, they were eating and drinking, marrying and giving in marriage, until the day that Noah entered the ark and did not know until the flood came and took them all away, so also will the coming of the Son of Man be. Then two men will be in the field: one will be taken and the other left. Two women will be grinding at the mill: one will be taken and the other left. Watch therefore, for you do not know what hour your Lord is coming. But know this, that if the master of the house had known what hour the thief would come, he would have watched and not allowed his house to be broken into. Therefore you also be ready, for the Son of Man is coming at an hour you do not expect." Other verses of the Bible that support this are 1 Thessalonians 4:16-17, and in 1 Corinthians 15: 51-55 we see that this whole process will take a split second," *In a Twinkling of a Eye"* (No Time to Repent and Receive Jesus as Lord). Some may say this is wrong. Even though God loves us, you must understand God has been calling you your whole life. And the age of graces in which I'm writing was 1,970 plus years long. Restoration of the whole world will happen and it will start with God removing the Church.

2 Peter 3: 9-13 sums it up. "The Lord is not slack concerning His promise, as some count slackness, but is long-suffering toward us, not willing that any should perish but that all should come to repentance. But the day of the Lord will come as a thief in the night, in which the heavens will pass away with a great noise, and the elements will melt with fervent

heat; both the earth and the works that are in it will be burned up. Therefore, since all things will be dissolved, what manner of persons ought you to be in holy conduct and godliness, looking for and hastening the coming of the day of God, because of which the heavens will be dissolved, being on fire, and the elements will melt with fervent heat? Nevertheless we according to His promise, look for a new heaven and a new earth in which righteousness dwells."

In the next Chapters I will write as if the rapture has happened. The sad reality is that only a fraction of the world population will make the greatest event to hit the world in over 2000 years: The Rapture of the Church. Below are some of the reasons why.

1. Pride of Life, 1 John 2:16
2. Money, Things, Too Busy, Matthew 16:26
3. Intellect & Rationalizations, Proverbs 3:5-7
4. Unbelief, Hebrews 11:6
5. Lovers of Evil, John 3:19

4. Receive Me Now

Millions are missing all over the world; you are now in the Great Tribulation Period. I can only imagine the mass amounts of horror; disasters and pain people are going through. In my mind's eye, I see thousands of accidents happening all over the world where Christians were driving, flying aircrafts, or operating equipment. The economy will suffer and knowledge will be lost because multitudes of people are missing.

I will give you some basic information on the time and period you now find yourself in (The Great Tribulation). It's important that you find a Bible and start to learn all you can about the Lord. The book of Revelation will give you accounts of future events to take place. I will attempt to keep you on point with some helpful hints from this book, but first things first.

This is a time to keep your head and try not to panic. There are some things you can do.

To the reader of this book, it's important for you to realize that you can still be saved, and even though you were not obedient to do the thing God was calling you to do, or perhaps you just didn't believe in God or his word, the Bible, you must now take a stand for God even if it means death. To gain eternal life on this side of the rapture means you may have to loose your life. God gave us mercy and grace before the rapture (in the Age of Grace) but that's out the window now. God still loves you and wants to have a relationship with you. One of the purposes of tribulation is to get mankind to repent and follow Christ no matter what. This is not the time to become angry or bitter towards God. Remember He's right. Our job is to turn from sin and humble ourselves, 2 Chronicles 7:22.

Say this prayer now and mean it in your heart, find all your loved ones and become a witness for God. I confess with my mouth that Jesus is Lord and that He died on the cross for my sins, and I believe in my heart that God raised him from the dead on the third day for my justification. I do now receive Him as my Lord and Savior. Amen.

5. Trials and Tribulations

Tribulations will consist of a series of events that will go from bad to worse. Wars, famine, martyred people; earthquakes, hail, fire and plagues are just some of the things that will happen during this terrible time. It is God's judgment on mankind. The Bible calls them **Seals** Judgments, Rev. 6:1; **Trumpets** Judgments, Rev 8:7; and **Bowl** Judgments, Rev.16: 1-21. These will happen all over the world and are designed to get your attention. You will have to make a decision for Christ or the Antichrist. God still wants millions of people to receive Christ. But this will come at a great a price. Many will be killed or become martyrs for the witness of Jesus. Revelation 6:9-11 reads "When He opened the fifth seal, I saw under the altar the souls of those who had been slain for the word of God and for the testimony which they held. And they cried with a loud voice, saying,' " "How Long, o Lord, holy and true, until you judge and avenge our blood on those who dwell on the earth? Then a white robe was given to each of them; and it was said to them that they should rest a little while longer, until both the number of their fellow servants and brethren, who would be killed as they were, completed. You must be strong and have faith in what God's word is saying to you. It's true. To gain everlasting life in heaven with God and your love ones, you must be a witness for the Lord even if it means losing your life for the sake of the gospel being preached.

Tribulations will last 7 years. Daniel 9:27 said "Then he shall confirm a covenant with many for one week; But in the middle of the week he shall bring an end to sacrifice and offering. And on the wing of abominations shall be one who makes desolate. Even until the consummation, which is determined, is poured out on the desolate."

Abomination = Anger, Rage, and Fury.
Desolate=Deserted, Isolated, Bleak, Uninhabitable,

To break down Daniel 9:27, the antichrist will sign a peace treaty with Israel for seven years, a treaty he will break in 3 1/2 years or 42 months.

It's important to know the characters that will play a roll in the end time events and how to identify them.

Satan has always tried to counterfeit the things of God; God's trinity is The Farther, Son and Holy Spirit. (God the Father, Jesus the Son of God, and the Holy Spirit) Satan has a false trinity, they are listed below.

Satan - Is a Fallen angel who leads fallen angels and demons. He is also know as Dragon, Devil, Serpent, Adversary, and Lucifer (Pure evil).

Antichrist - Signs a covenant with Israel for seven years, and will break it in 31/2 or 42 months. (A government official from somewhere in the world) He is also know as the Beast.

False Prophet - Will head the one world church during the Tribulation. He will advocate on the behalf of the Antichrist, He causes all, both small and great, rich and poor, free and slave, to receive a mark. (A spiritual leader of some kind)

Revelations 13: 15-17 said "He was granted power to give breath to the image of the beast, that the image of the beast should both speak and cause as many as would not worship the image of the beast to be killed. He causes all, both small and great, rich and poor, free and slave, to receive a mark on their right hand or on their foreheads, and that no one may buy or sell except one who has the mark or the name of the beast, or the number of his name. Here is wisdom, let him who has understanding calculate the number of the beast, for it is the number of a man: His number is 666."

This is a terrible time to be on earth. It is a time of great control by the enemy. Everyone who finds their self in this period, even the very rich, will have to submit to Satan and his followers or loss their lives. Bibles are probably being burned to keep people from the truth. People are dieing because they are taking a stand for Jesus. This is important: Do not be afraid to die for Jesus, in the time in which you are living. You won't have years to do your own thing.

It is either Christ or the Antichrist. This is a time to stand up and be a witness. If you go underground, go underground for the Lord, win people to Christ. The following verses from the Bible will help you understand.

2 Thessalonians 2:8-12 "And then the lawless one will be revealed whom the Lord will consume with the brightness of his coming. The Coming of the Lawless one is according to the working of Satan, with all power, signs, and lying wonders, and with all unrighteous deception among those who perish, because they did not receive the love of the truth, that they might be saved. And for this reason God will send them strong delusion, that they should believe the lie. That they all may be condemned who did not believe the truth but had pleasure in unrighteousness."

This is a time of great deception and lies. It's evident that God is not happy with those who sought after the pleasures of sin over a life of holiness. As I said before in the beginning of this book, God does not expect you to be perfect, but He does want you to have a "want to" attitude. He is God and can see your heart. During the Age of Grace God had much compassion for such a person but now it's clear that a decision for Christ will be much harder because of deception and lies. The following is a list of the major judgments God will pour out on a rebellious world in the order in which they will happen.

Seal Judgment Rev. 6:1-17, Rev. 7:1-15, Rev. 8:1-5

- 1st. Seal White Horse has power to conquer.
- 2nd. Seal - Conflicts and Death
- 3rd. Seal - Famine and Lack
- 4th. Seal - Killings, hunger, and death by beast of the earth.
- 5th. Seal - The cry of the martyrs (people who were slain for Christ).

- 6th. Seal - Cosmic Activity, (stars falling to earth)
- 7th. Seal - Silence followed by thundering, lightnings and earthquakes.

Trumpet Judgments Rev. 8:7-13, Rev. 9:1-21, Rev. 11:15-19

- 1st. Trumpet - Third of the trees burned up.
- 2nd. Trumpet - A third of living creatures in the sea die.
- 3rd. Trumpet - Many die because a third of rivers and springs become bitter.
- 4th. Trumpet - A third of the day will not shine, and likewise the night.
- 5th. Trumpet - Torment for five months from a locust with teeth and a tail like scorpions.
- 6th. Trumpet - A third of man kind killed by plagues.
- 7th. Trumpet - The Kingdom proclaimed.

Bowl Judgments Rev. 16:1-21

- 1st Bowl - People who worship the image or who have the mark of the beast will have loathsome sores. (Loathsome means detestable.)
- 2nd. Bowl - Sea turns to blood, every living creature in the sea dies.
- 3rd. Bowl - Rivers and springs turn to blood.
- 4th. Bowl - Men are scorched by the sun.
- 5th. Bowl - Darkness and Pain
- 6th. Bowl - River Euphrates dries up, so kings from the east could cross it to make war. (Armageddon)
- 7th. Bowl - Thundering and lightning's, a mighty earthquake, islands and mountains are not found and great hail from heaven.

God will destroy the evil world system that he calls Babylon the Great, a system that was a dwelling place of demons, a prison for every foul spirit. Rev. 18: 1-24

6. Victory In Jesus

As I read through the 21 judgments, there was a phrase I saw over and over again, and it said, "They did not repent of their sins." The judgments in the Book of Revelations should cause one to bow down before God. If you are one who becomes angry and bitter, and refuses to repent, there is no victory or good new for you. However there is victory for the one who submits and turns to the Lord.

No matter what you think about our Lord God Almighty and his perfect plan of redemption and restoration, when it is all said and done, Heaven will be filled with people who want to be there. The person that trusted God even though they didn't fully understand, the person who by faith received the free gift of his son, Jesus Christ, and the person that said yes to the Holy Spirit, as He molded and shaped their lives.

This book was created to encourage you through a terrible time. If there are Bibles around, familiarize yourself with the scriptures in Revelations. Shortly after the last bowl judgment Jesus is coming, this is called the Second Coming.

Rev. 19:11-16 "Now I saw heaven open, and behold, a white horse. And He who sat on him was called faithful and true, and in righteousness He judges and makes war. His eyes were like a flame of fire, and on his head were many crowns. He had a name written that no one knew except Himself. He was clothed with a robe dipped in blood, and His name is called The Word of God. And the armies in heaven clothed in fine linen, white and clean, Followed Him on white horses. Now out of his mouth goes a sharp sword, that with it He should strike the nations. And He Himself will rule them with a rod of iron. He Himself treads the winepress of the fierceness and wrath of the almighty God. And He has on His robe and on His thigh a name written:

KING OF KING AND LORDS OF LORDS.

I've heard the statement, "we win in the end" all my Christian life. I will start to sum up this book with that very idea in mind. The following bullet points show the future events of a winning team.

Rev. 19:20-21 "Then the beast was captured and with him the false prophet who worked signs in his presence, by which he deceived those who received the mark of the beast and those who worshiped his image. These two were cast alive into the lake of fire burning with brimstone. And the rest were killed with the sword, which proceeded from the mouth of Him who sat on the horse. And all the birds were filled with their flesh."

Rev. 20:1-3 "Then I saw an angel coming down from heaven, having the key to the bottomless pit and great chain in his hand. He laid hold of the dragon, that serpent of old, who is the Devil and Satan, and bound him for a thousand years; and he cast him into the bottomless pit, and shut him up, and set a seal on him, so he should deceive the nations no more till the thousand years were finished. But after these things he must be released for a little while.'"

Rev. 20:4-6 "And I saw thrones, and they sat on them, and judgment was committed to them. Then I saw the souls of those who had been beheaded for their witness to Jesus and for the word of God, who had not received his mark on their foreheads or on their hands. And they lived and reigned with Christ for a thousand years. But the rest of the dead did not live again until the thousand years were finished. This is the first resurrection."

We are in the last chapters of the Bible and the last dispensation since the world began - The 1000-year Millennial Kingdom. God has always wanted you to freely choose him, to trust him, and reverence him. Even now your free will is intact. The devil will be loosed once more to deceive the nations. Stay true to God and enter into all he has for you. (This is only a test.)

Gog and Magog - The name of a final battle God will have with Satan.

Rev. 20:7-10 "Now when the thousand years have expired, Satan will be released from his prison and will go out to deceive the nations which are in the four corners of the earth, Gog and Magog, to gather them together to battle, whose numbers is as the sand of the sea. They went up on the breadth of the earth and surrounded the camp of the saints and the beloved city. And fire came down from God out of heaven and devoured them. The devil, who deceived them, was cast into the lake of fire and brimstone where the beast and false prophet are. **And they will be tormented day and night forever and ever.**

There is a judgment that will come to those who refused to obey Gods word and accept his Son Jesus as Lord and Savior. It's called the Great White Throne Judgment. God's word said "Nor is there salvation in any other. For there is no other name under heaven given among men by which we must be saved." Acts 4:12. If wide is the gate that leads to destruction, that means millions, perhaps billions, of people will find that their names are not in the Book of Life. Because they thought they were good enough, that surely God won't reject me just because I rejected him and his Son and did my own thing. There will be those who thought once you were dead, you were dead. Not true. God's Word tells us there is an everlasting life for the believers, John 3:16, John 17:2-3 and an everlasting punishment for those who reject Christ, Matt 25:46. In 2 Thessalonians 1:8-9 in the New Testament, God's Word reads "in flaming fire taking vengeance on those who do not know God, and on those who do not obey the gospel of our Lord Jesus Christ. These shall be punished with everlasting destruction from the presence of the Lord and from the glory of His power. To the reader of this book you want your name in the Book of Life. Stop rationalizing in your mind, drop the pride, humble yourself, this thing is real. Accept Gods gift he's trying to give you. Stop compromising your life, let go of this world and this world system. Fall to your knees and ask God to forgive you of your sin. Rev. 20:11-15 reads, "Then I saw a great white throne and Him who sat on it, from whose face the earth and the heaven fled away. And there was found no place for them. And I saw the dead, small and great, standing before God, and books were opened. And another book was opened, which is the Book of Life. And the dead were judged according to their works, by the things, which were written in the books. The sea gave up the dead who where in it and the Death and Hades delivered up the dead who were in them. And they were judged, each one according to his works. The Death and Hades were cast into the lake of fire. This is the second death. And anyone not found written in the Book of Life was cast into the lake of fire."

Our Lord and Savior loves you very much and if you will trust Him, He will deal with all that comes against you, even you. Trust is the key to your victory. Get rid of your plans. In the days in which you now find yourself, His plan is far better and works. The Lord in His Word said He has given everything that pertains to life and Godliness. When you stand before God, you will have no excuses for your actions or lack of actions. He gave His Word that you might have the victory. Our Lord has a perfect plan for your life in Heaven, back to Eden the way it was suppose to be in the beginning.

Rev. 21:1-8 reads "Now I saw a new heaven and a new earth, for the first heaven and the first earth had passed away. Also there was no sea. Then I, John, saw the holy City, New Jerusalem, coming down out of heaven from God, prepared as a bride adorned for her husband. And I heard a loud voice from heaven saying, 'Behold, the tabernacle of God is with men, and He will dwell with them, and they shall be His people. God Himself will be with them and be their God. And God will wipe away every tear from their eyes; there shall be no more death, nor sorrow, nor crying. There shall be no more pain, for the former things have passed away.' Then He who sat on the throne said, 'Behold, I make all things new' And He said to me, 'Write, for these words are true and faithful.' And He said to me, 'It is done! I am the Alpha and the Omega, the Beginning and the End. I will give of the fountain of the water of life freely to him who thirsts. He who overcomes shall inherit all things, and I will be his God and he shall be my son. But the cowardly, unbelieving, abominable, murderers, sexually immoral, sorcerers, idolaters, and all liars shall have their part in the lake which burns with fire and brimstone, which is the second death."

The last word in the Bible is AMEN. That word means, "so be it". For the one who uses it, I agree with you Lord. Yes, have your way. God is always calling you and I to take that next step of faith, Rev. 22:20-21 reads, "He who testifies to these things says, 'Surly I am coming quickly.' Amen. Even so, come, Lord Jesus! The grace of our Lord Jesus Christ be with you all. Amen."

Special Thanks

Heavenly Father = Source

Demetria King = Wife

Kendra King = Cover graphic

Kathy Weiss = Editing

Bryce Goff = Editing

Karissa Wheeler = Daughter

Gatekeeper Press = Editing/Publishing

www.ingramcontent.com/pod-product-compliance
Lightning Source LLC
LaVergne TN
LVHW021738060526
838200LV00052B/3336